A BRIEF ILLUSTRATED
HISTORY of
LIFE ON EARTH

STEVE PARKER
&
DAVID WEST

CAPSTONE PRESS
a capstone imprint

First published in hardcover by Capstone Press, an imprint of Capstone, in 2017
1710 Roe Crest Drive, North Mankato, Minnesota 56003
www.mycapstone.com

Library of Congress Cataloging-in-Publication Data
Names: Parker, Steve, 1952- author.
Title: A brief illustrated history of life on Earth / by Steve Parker.
Description: North Mankato, Minnesota : Capstone Press, [2017] | Series: Fact
finders. A brief illustrated history | Audience: Ages 8-11. | Audience:
Grades 4 to 6. | Includes bibliographical references and index.
Identifiers: LCCN 2016032626 |
ISBN 9781515725213 (library binding)
Subjects: LCSH: Evolution (Biology)—Juvenile literature. | Life (Biology)—Juvenile literature.
Classification: LCC QH367.1 .P35 2017 | DDC 576.8—dc23
LC record available at https://lccn.loc.gov/2016032626

A BRIEF ILLUSTRATED HISTORY OF LIFE ON EARTH
was produced by
David West Children's Books, 6 Princeton Court, 55 Felsham Road, London SW15 1AZ

Designed and illustrated by David West
Text by Steve Parker
Editor Brenda Haugen

Printed in China
007966

TABLE OF CONTENTS

INTRODUCTION

ABOUT 4.6 BILLION YEARS AGO, THE SUN, EARTH, AND OTHER BODIES in the Solar System began to form from clouds of gas and dust whirling in space. Conditions on the young Earth, such as choking gases and fierce rays from the new Sun, raging storms, volcanoes, and earthquakes made life on Earth impossible. But the planet gradually cooled and calmed. By 3.5 billion years ago, early life appeared as microscopic jelly-like specks in the sea.

Living things, or organisms, remained small and simple for another 2 billion years. However there were changing conditions in the air and water. By 1 billion years ago, this allowed larger organisms to thrive and diversify. At first they were mostly plants, growing with the energy of sunlight. Then, from 540 million years ago, a rapid "explosion" in animal life occurred. Creatures became bigger and more complex, to eat the new plants—and each other. Changes have followed ever since, as life adapted to Earth's always-changing habitats and environments.

Charles Darwin
1809–1882

Darwin and the ages of life
In 1859 English naturalist Charles Darwin explained how life adapts to changing conditions, with the theory of evolution by natural selection. Evolution has happened throughout Earth's immense history (right). The history of Earth is divided into major units called eons, such as the Hadean, when the environment was too harsh for life. Then the Archean and Proterozoic eons saw microlife in water. Next came the Palaeozoic, Mesozoic, and Cenozoic eras, when most major groups of living things appeared. Human evolution's history is almost invisible at this scale.

Prokaryotes and eukaryotes
Prokaryotes are the simplest organisms, with most parts inside the single cell floating freely. Eukaryotes are more organized, with the genetic material DNA and other contents wrapped in skin-like membrane packages. Eukaryotes started as single cells, which then gathered into multicelled plants and animals.

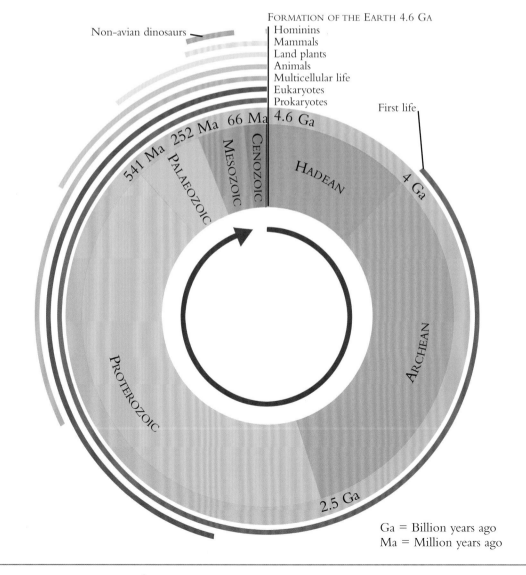

Non-avian dinosaurs

FORMATION OF THE EARTH 4.6 GA
Hominins
Mammals
Land plants
Animals
Multicellular life
Eukaryotes
Prokaryotes

First life

541 Ma 252 Ma 66 Ma 4.6 Ga

PALAEOZOIC
MESOZOIC
CENOZOIC
HADEAN
4 Ga

PROTEROZOIC

ARCHEAN

2.5 Ga

Ga = Billion years ago
Ma = Million years ago

One billion years after Earth formed, the surroundings became suitable for the first life-forms. They probably arose in the warm, shallow edges of seas, where lightning storms provided energy for minerals and nutrients gradually to gather into living cells.

PROTEROZOIC TO CAMBRIAN
2.5 BILLION—485 MILLION YEARS AGO

THE PROTEROZOIC EON LASTED NEARLY 2 BILLION YEARS—ALMOST HALF OF EARTH'S ENTIRE EXISTENCE. TINY REMAINS CALLED MICROFOSSILS SHOW THAT LIFE THRIVED IN WATER BUT NOT ON LAND. AS THE PROTEROZOIC EON GAVE WAY TO THE CAMBRIAN PERIOD, 541 MILLION YEARS AGO, THE BIGGEST EVENT ALL IN LIFE'S HISTORY OCCURRED—THE "CAMBRIAN EXPLOSION."

Stromatolites, rocky mounds of microorganisms, grew in shallow Proterozoic seas.

Much evidence for the history of life comes from fossils of plants, animals, and other organisms preserved in rocks and "turned to stone." Soft-bodied organisms rot and decay quickly and so their fossils are rare. Fossils show that during most of the Proterozoic, life-forms were smaller than the dot on this "i," each one a single cell. By 600 million years ago, bigger organisms began to appear as collections of cells. Steadily they evolved larger and more complex bodies.

The last period of the Proterozoic, the Ediacaran (635 to 541 million years ago), is named after fossils from the Ediacara Hill, South Australia. By this time whole communities of soft-bodied plants and animals lived in warm, shallow seas. Some resembled seaweeds. Others were sponge- or worm-shaped bottom-dwellers or jellyfish-like drifters. Their fossils are faint and rare. Many were unfamiliar and difficult to group with today's plants and creatures.

A pair of Anomalocaris *hunt trilobites some 505 million years ago. Their Cambrian seabed is now the Rocky Mountains of British Columbia, Canada.*

Trilobite

"Trilobite" means "three-lobed" and comes from the three body parts (left, central, and right) divided by two long furrows. Many were seabed scavengers, sifting the mud for food.

Some were plant-eaters or predators. Trilobites had crescent-shaped head shields, bodies of many similar sections, or segments, and numerous walking legs underneath. The largest grew to almost 2.5 feet (75 cm) long. *Anomalocaris,* a hunter of trilobites,

Anomalocaris

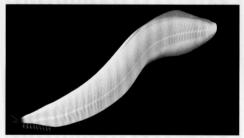

Pikaia

had large eyes for excellent vision. *Pikaia* was 2 inches (5 cm) long, swam like an eel, and could have been an early stage in the evolution of vertebrates, or backboned animals.

The next period, the Cambrian, saw rapid evolution of many new forms, including the first big predators. Largest was fearsome *Anomalocaris*, more than 3.3 feet (1 meter) long. Events during this "Cambrian explosion" are well known because animals evolved new, hard body features such as shells, claws, and spines. These were much more likely to fossilize. Within 25 million years—the blink of an eye in terms of

life's history—about 30 of the 40-plus major animal groups, or phyla, known today, were established. They included the simplest animals, sponges; cnidarians such as anemones and corals; tough-shelled molluscs such as sea-snails and ammonites; early kinds of sea urchins, sea-lilies, and other echinoderms; and vast numbers of arthropods—creatures with hard body casings and jointed legs.

The first big group of arthropods was trilobites. They are among the most long-lasting and numerous of all extinct creatures. Trilobites first appeared some 520 million years ago, evolved into more than 15,000 kinds or species, and only died out 250 million years ago. Like many Cambrian organisms, their widespread fossils show they lived in seas around the world.

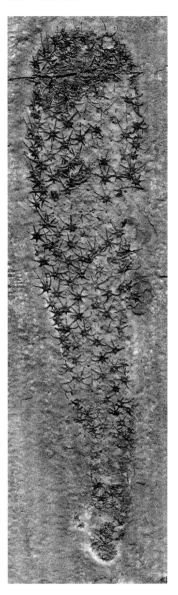

Chancelloria, 3 inches (7 centimeters) tall had features of both sponges and molluscs.

Opabinia

Opabinia, one of the strangest animals in Cambrian oceans, had five eyes, a long bendy proboscis (like a trunk), and a spiky mouth. Like many creatures of the time it was small.

Only 2.5 inches (6.5 cm) long, *Opabinia* may have been a cousin of today's velvet-worms. *Ottoia*, another animal that burrowed in the seabed, was up to 4 inches (10 cm) long and belonged to the priapulid or cactus

Ottoia *fossil*

worm group. Its flexible proboscis had sharp spines and hooks that reached out to grab prey. Priapulids or cactus worms still survive today.

living cactus worm

ORDOVICIAN TO SILURIAN
485—419 MILLION YEARS AGO

THE ORDOVICIAN PERIOD SAW A DRAMATIC INCREASE IN THE NUMBERS AND KINDS OF LIVING THINGS IN WATER—IN SEAS, AND ALSO RIVERS AND LAKES. AS CONTINENTS DRIFTED AROUND THE GLOBE, WARM, NUTRIENT-RICH SHALLOW SEAS BECAME MORE WIDESPREAD, ENCOURAGING YET MORE EVOLUTION. DURING THE NEXT PERIOD, SILURIAN, PLANTS AND THEN ANIMALS SPREAD ONTO LAND.

Orthoceras, *6 inches (15 cm) long, belonged to the nautiloid mollusc group. They were similar to their modern cousins, squid.*

Jawless, finless fish avoid Pterygotus *in the Silurian shallows. Related to today's horseshoe crabs, this eurypterid was a major predator at 5.3 feet (1.6 m) long.*

The shallow seas of the Ordovician (485 to 444 million years ago) were home to many new kinds of animals, as well as early reef-based communities of sponges, corals, and shellfish molluscs. All were prey for the massive eurypterids or sea scorpions. Above them swam more big, fierce predators such as curly-shelled ammonites and straight-shelled nautiloids. Another new group of creatures also appeared—vertebrates. At first vertebrates were small, rare, and lacked jaws, but as fish, they would soon dominate the seas.

Some of the first living reef habitats were formed by molluscs with a two-part shell, called bivalves.

fossilized bivalves from the Ordovician seabed

Even 450 million years ago they were already similar to their modern cousins, mussels and clams. As they died, their empty shells piled up to form crags and caves which became new habitats for other creatures to exploit. Other reef-builders included echinoderms such as crinoids. Eurypterids were the dominant Ordovician predators and the largest arthropods ever known, some reaching 8 feet (2.5 m) in length.

They persisted until the greatest of all mass extinctions at the end of the Permian Period, 252 million years ago.

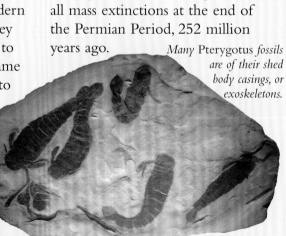

Many Pterygotus *fossils are of their shed body casings, or exoskeletons.*

At the end of the Ordovician continental drift, mass volcanic eruptions and other changes caused global cooling. This led to the first of the "Big Five" mass extinctions that have affected life on Earth.

Many corals, trilobites, molluscs, and others disappeared over some 20 million years. However the event left habitats ready for the evolution of new life-forms during the Silurian (444 to 419 million years ago).

A major new vertebrate group was the jawed fishes. The backbone and fins allowed them to swim fast and maneuver well, while the jaws soon became adapted to different roles, such as scavenging, eating plants, and biting prey.

Life's invasion of the land was slow. It started perhaps 500 million years ago with microscopic organisms such as blue-green algae, also called cyanobacteria, which coated rocks at the water's edge. Gradually aquatic plants developed waterproof coverings and bodies stiffened with strong tubes, so they could survive just above the waterline. Small herbivores such as worms and arthropods evolved waterproofing and followed them. The end of the Silurian saw land carnivores, arthropods as small as this "O" that became mites, centipedes, and spiders.

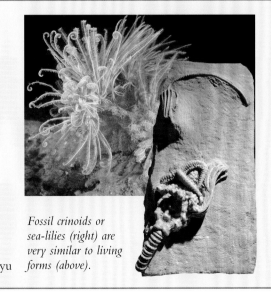

Cooksonia *was one of the first land plants 430 million years ago.*

head shield of the galeaspid jawless fish, Laxaspis

The earliest fish were small, lacked fins or jaws, and wriggled clumsily along the seabed. The sucker-like mouth filtered seabed ooze and mud and ate soft prey such as worms. Some, such as the Silurian galeaspids, evolved strong, shield-like heads and body armor as defense against eurypterids. The next great advance was jaws to capture and cut up prey and also defend against enemies. By the end of the Silurian, jawed, finned, bony fish such as *Guiyu*, about 12 inches (30 cm) in length, were firmly established.

bony fish Guiyu

Fossil crinoids or sea-lilies (right) are very similar to living forms (above).

9

DEVONIAN
419—359 MILLION YEARS AGO

Some of the most important changes in the history of life occurred during the Devonian Period. Major new groups of fish appeared, including the ancestors of tetrapods (four-legged, backboned land animals). Out of the water, plants also evolved into important new groups, and land habitats and animals began to diversify rapidly.

Orcanthus *chases a lungfish,* Scaumenacia, *as two* Dipterus *lungfish escape. This "spiny shark" was related to true sharks.*

The Devonian is sometimes called the "Age of Fishes." There were fish before and after, but this was the time they truly dominated the sea, long before mammals such as seals, dolphins, and whales. Jawed, finned fish evolved rapidly into new kinds. Some still survive today, such as sharks with cartilage skeletons, and bony fish including the speedy ray-fins and the lobe-fins with muscular limb bases. Other Devonian fish died out, such as the armored placoderms, and the acanthodians or "spiny sharks."

Devonian oceans swarmed with established invertebrates such as jellyfish and corals, sea scorpions and other arthropods, and ammonites and their mollusc cousins. A large group of fish from the Silurian that continued to flourish were heterostracans. They lacked jaws and proper fins, although some had tails and body parts drawn out into flaps. Stiff skin plates and scales gave protection but made them heavy. Most heterostracans were slow swimmers and fed on

Drepanaspis, *an 8 inches (20 cm) long heterostracan*

the placoderm Bothriolepis

Pteraspis

Doryapsis

small, soft-bodied prey. *Drepanaspis* was ray-shaped, and *Doryaspis*, 6 inches (15 cm) long, had a spiky snout. *Pteraspis*, at 8 inches (20 cm), was streamlined and had side and back spines. The heterostracan group died out at the end of the Devonian.

The land saw even greater changes. Small early plants, mostly less than 1 foot (30 cm) tall, developed new, improved features. These included better waterproofing and stiff fibers to hold their stems upright away from swampy water and ground-based herbivore animals. Other features

Dunkleosteus—here hunting early sharks—was 33 feet (10 m) long and the biggest Devonian predator.

were big leaves to catch more sunlight, and seed-like spores to spread widely. Such plants included ferns and clubmosses still living today, and several similar groups that went extinct. Some of these reached heights of 33 feet (10 m) and formed the first forests.

These big land plants dropped plentiful leaves into already weed-rich swamps and rivers. Here some lobe-fin fish—with a "stump" of muscle at the base of each fin—evolved more muscle and less fin, forming limbs with finger-like digits. The main reason was probably to push and crawl through the dense water plants. Also swamps have little oxygen dissolved in the water, so these fish gradually developed lungs to replace gills. The new, muscular limbs could lift the fish's head out of the water, to breathe—and also to feed on small land animals.

Two Acanthostega *crawl among* Wattieza tree-ferns, *26 feet (8 m) tall.*

Dunkleosteus

Rhizodus

The fiercest of Devonian fish were placoderms, "plated-skins," such as huge *Dunkleosteus* and the smaller *Bothriolepis*. They had strong bony plates over the head and front body, which in *Dunkleosteus* formed jagged tooth blades. Another massive predator was *Rhizodus*, reaching 23 feet (7 m) in length.

It hunted in freshwater lakes and rivers. It was a lobe-fin fish, related to today's lungfish. Other lobe-fins began to evolve limbs. One was *Acanthostega*, which lived in swamps

Archaeopteris

and grew to 2 feet (60 cm). Its front limbs had eight digits or "toes." Similar fish would evolve into the first four-limbed land animals, tetrapods, that hunted among the early forests of giant fern-like trees such as *Wattieza* and *Archaeopteris*.

CARBONIFEROUS
359—299 MILLION YEARS AGO

L IFE HAS PROBABLY NEVER FLOURISHED SO MUCH ON LAND AS DURING THE CARBONIFEROUS PERIOD. FORESTS OF TREE-FERNS AND OTHER PLANTS THRIVED IN WARM SWAMPS. INSECTS AND OTHER NEW ARTHROPODS ABOUNDED. AMPHIBIANS FLOURISHED. ANOTHER NEW GROUP OF VERTEBRATES APPEARED, ALTHOUGH AS YET SMALL AND SCARCE—REPTILES.

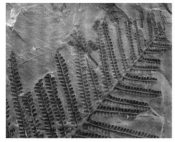

The fern Pecopteris *left exceptionally plentiful fossils.*

Earth's world climate was warm and moist, with few seasonal changes. Rivers, lakes, and swamps covered much of the land. Studies of rocks and minerals formed at the time show air contained almost one-third oxygen, compared to today's one-fifth. All these conditions encouraged plants to spread widely and grow huge. Massive ferns, scale-trees, clubmosses, and horsetails crowded the landscape. They reproduced by spores, which lack a food store for the baby plant. But, among the new plants were seed-ferns, each seed containing a food store—one of plant evolution's great successes. Dead plants rotted slowly, piled up, fossilized and became coal, a rock containing plentiful carbon that gave the period its name.

In a steamy Carboniferous "coal swamp," the giant millipede Arthropleura *rears up, surprised by the early amphibian* Eogyrinus. *Smaller amphibians* Dendrerpeton *swim away as the massive dragonfly-like* Meganeura *flaps above.*

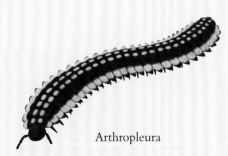

Arthropleura

Many land invertebrates of the Carboniferous were cousins of today's groups, rather than direct ancestors. *Arthropleura* was up to 8 feet (2.5 m) in length and, like living millipedes, a harmless

herbivore or detritivore, eating rotting remains on the forest floor. *Meganeura* was a griffinfly—a relative of dragonflies, and a similar speedy aerial hunter. *Dendrerpeton*, up to 3.3 feet (1 m) long, belonged to

Meganeura's wings spanned 2.3 feet (70 cm).

Dendrerpeton

a now-extinct amphibian group known as temnospondyls. They survived for more than 200 million years and adapted to many land and freshwater habitats, but were mostly gone by 150 million years ago.

The vast forests of huge plants were home to worms of many species, and early snail-like land molluscs. Among the arthropods were many groups of insects, such as ancient cousins of cockroaches and dragonflies, the first members of the spider group, the arachnids, as well as the centipedes. The first big land creature was the millipede-like *Arthropleura*.

The first land-walking vertebrates also appeared, the amphibians. They evolved from fish that developed limbs, known as "fishapods." But they did not have fully waterproof skin or eggs, so they had to stay near water. However, near the end of the Carboniferous, some amphibians gave rise to the first reptiles, such as the 8 inches (20 cm) long, lizard-shaped *Hylonomus*. Their scaly skin and hard-shelled eggs at last freed them from the necessity of living in or near the water.

At the end of the Carboniferous, a huge holocephalian Edestus *chases* Mesosaurus, *a reptile newly adapting to sea life.*

In seas and oceans, invertebrates such as ammonites, sea scorpions, and sea-lilies thrived worldwide. Trilobites were fading. Bony fish gradually became more widespread, and faster. They were still rivalled in size by cartilage-skeleton fish such as true sharks and also the holocephalians. This last group survives today as the little-known ratfish or chimaeras, mostly in the deep sea.

Some Carboniferous amphibians became giants, such as *Eogyrinus* at 16 feet (5 m) long. It had a broad, long tail for fast swimming but its limbs were relatively weak. It probably hunted mainly in water for prey such as small fish, although, like a crocodile, it could lunge onto land to grab victims. Like all amphibians, *Eogyrinus* lived in fresh water. In the sea, its role as a medium-large predator was taken by various fish. The holocephalian *Edestus* reached 20 feet (6 m). Mainly its teeth are known from fossils, so its body size and shape are estimated from today's ratfish. Smaller at 3.3 feet (1 m) was *Mesosaurus*, one of the first newly evolved reptiles to adapt to sea life. The shark *Stethacanthus*, 2.3 feet (70 cm) long, had an extraordinary dorsal fin shaped like an anvil.

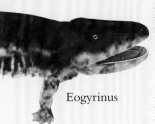

Eogyrinus

Edestus

Mesosaurus

Stethacanthus

PERMIAN
299—252 MILLION YEARS AGO

THE PERMIAN PERIOD CONTRASTED GREATLY WITH THE PREVIOUS CARBONIFEROUS. ALL THE WORLD'S LAND MASSES HAD DRIFTED TOGETHER TO FORM THE SUPERCONTINENT OF PANGEA. DRY LANDS AND DESERTS SPREAD ACROSS ITS CENTER AS THE CLIMATE BECAME DRIER AND MORE CHANGEABLE, WITH WARM AND COOL SEASONS. THIS CHANGE HAD A PROFOUND EFFECT ON LIFE.

The drying Permian climate meant the "Age of Amphibians" slowly faded, and instead encouraged animals that could survive with little water. Among them were many large, scaly vertebrates that laid waterproof-shelled eggs, known by the general name of amniotes. Many looked like reptiles, but they were not actually reptilian, because they had a different pattern of openings in the skull bone. One of these groups was the synapsids. Early forms are known as pelycosaurs, such as sail-backed predator *Dimetrodon* and its similar-looking herbivore cousin *Edaphosaurus*. With its long, sharp, fang-shaped teeth, *Dimetrodon* was the first truly big, fearsome land predator. It grew to around 15 feet (4.5 m) long and weighed more than 550 pounds (250 kilograms).

Diplocaulus, a strange amphibian, had a "boomerang" head shape.

Dimetrodon catches the desert sun's evening rays with its sail to stay warm and active. Two Eryops amphibians try to survive in their waterhole—a shrinking habitat in the drying Permian.

Synapsids were among the main large land animals of the Permian. Most had wide bodies with legs that sprawled out sideways, as in most reptiles (but not dinosaurs). One of the biggest was *Cotylorhyncus*, from 275 million years ago, at 13 feet (4 m) long and weighing 1.1 tons (1 metric ton). It had plant-chopping teeth, and its fossils come from what is now North America. In southern Africa slightly later, 260 million years ago, lived the similar-sized *Jonkeria*. Its large, pointed front teeth and smaller cheek teeth suggest it was more of an omnivore, eating plants and animals, or perhaps even a carnivore, attacking old or weak victims. The smaller herbivore *Moschops*, from southern Africa at the same time period, was 8 feet (2.5 m) long.

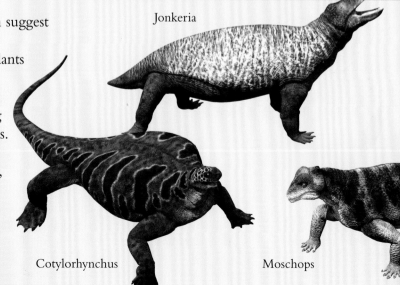

Jonkeria

Cotylorhynchus

Moschops

Saber-toothed Inostrancevia *watches a* Doliosauriscus *pack attack* Estemmenosuchus. *All these therapsids lived in Asia.*

Later in the Permian came the therapsids. Sometimes called "mammal-like reptiles," these synapsids were neither reptiles nor mammals.

However some were warm-blooded, had fur or hair, and may have given birth to babies rather than laying eggs. Therapsids were a rapid success, with hundreds of kinds evolving through the mid to late Permian. They had different lifestyles, from herbivores to carnivores and scavengers.

Even the therapsids were badly affected by the greatest of all mass extinctions at the end of the Permian Period, 252 million years ago. In the "Great Dying," possibly caused by volcanic activity, more than nine out of ten kinds of land animals died out, as well as vast numbers in the seas, including many ammonites and the last of the trilobites. Some large amphibians that had adapted to the drier Permian also died. Plants were likewise devastated. The event marked the end of the Palaeozoic Era, or "ancient life." Soon surviving therapsids became the first mammals, and an obscure group of reptiles evolved and later rose to dominance—the dinosaurs.

Three wolf-sized Lycaenops *chase* Lystrosaurus *in this therapsid late Permian scene based in southern Africa.*

Keratocephalus

Criocephalosaurus

Moschops belonged to the synapsid group known as dinocephalians, or "terrible heads," because of the very thick skull bone with lumps, bumps, and ridges. This may have been used in self defense to ram predators, and also headbutt rivals to win control of the group and breeding partners, as sheep and goats do today. Another southern African member was *Keratocephalus*, at 10 feet (3 m) long, with a heavy body that weighed up to 1.1 tons (1 metric ton). Its small, peg-shaped, sharp-ridged teeth show it was a herbivore, chopping up ferns and other plants that digested slowly in its huge gut. *Criocephalosaurus* was yet another dinocephalian from the same region, same time period, and similar in size to *Keratosaurus*. Mainly its skulls are known as fossils, so the rest of the body is estimated from other dinocephalians. How all these herbivores lived together in the same place and time is not clear, since in modern habitats, such similar creatures would compete for food, and only one or two would survive.

TRIASSIC
252—201 MILLION YEARS AGO

THE END-OF-PERMIAN MASS EXTINCTION LEFT FAR FEWER ANIMALS AND PLANTS AT THE START OF THE TRIASSIC. THERE WERE GREAT OPPORTUNITIES FOR SURVIVORS TO ADAPT INTO NEW HABITATS. THESE WERE ALSO CHANGING. THE CLIMATE IN THE INTERIOR OF PANGEA REMAINED LARGELY WARM AND DRY, BUT GRADUALLY BECAME MORE SEASONAL AND RAINY AROUND THE EDGES.

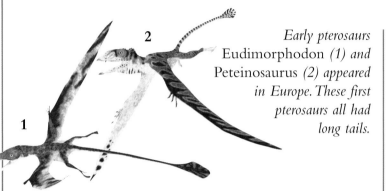

Early pterosaurs Eudimorphodon *(1) and* Peteinosaurus *(2) appeared in Europe. These first pterosaurs all had long tails.*

The main animals to flourish in the new conditions of the Triassic were reptiles. From small beginnings, they rapidly evolved into many types. Major new groups that lasted throughout the Mesozoic era included winged pterosaurs in the air, dinosaurs on land, and tubby-bodied plesiosaurs, and dolphin-shaped ichthyosaurs in the seas.

Other reptile groups were successful during the Triassic but quickly faded by its end. On land they included herbivorous rhyncosaurs; armored, plant-eating aetosaurs; and crocodile-like phytosaurs and rauisuchians. In the sea swam placodonts, some of which were lizard-shaped and thick-set while others were wide-bodied like turtles, and also the sleek, fish-hunting nothosaurs and true turtles.

All of these groups and more marked the Triassic as the beginning of the "Age of Reptiles."

In this coastal Triassic scene two Coelophysis *(1), slim and agile early dinosaurs, avoid the rauisuchian* Postosuchus *(2), which has already caught a shark,* Xenocanthus. *A crocodile-like phytosaur* Rutiodon *(3) watches from the water.* Desmatosuchus *(4), an aetosaur, ambles along the beach as two dicynodonts* Placerias *(5) wade past. Early relatives of mammals, cynodonts (6), seek safety up a tree. Of all these groups, only cynodonts and dinosaurs have surviving relatives.*

A wide array of new reptile groups spread across the Triassic landscape. Rhynchosaurs such as *Hyperodapedon* were "Triassic sheep," about the same size as today's sheep, and common herbivores in many habitats. They snipped off vegetation with sharp, beak-like mouths. Dicynodonts were also successful herbivores, with two tusk-like teeth. *Placerias*, as big as a modern cow, weighed over 1.1 tons (1 metric ton). Other plant-eaters included aetosaurs, such as the 17-foot (5-m) *Desmatosuchus*, with plates and spikes of bone in the skin.

Along with dinosaurs and others, they belonged to the archosaur group. *Plateosaurus* was the first really large dinosaur, 33 feet (10 m) in length and weighing 4.4 tons (4 metric tons).

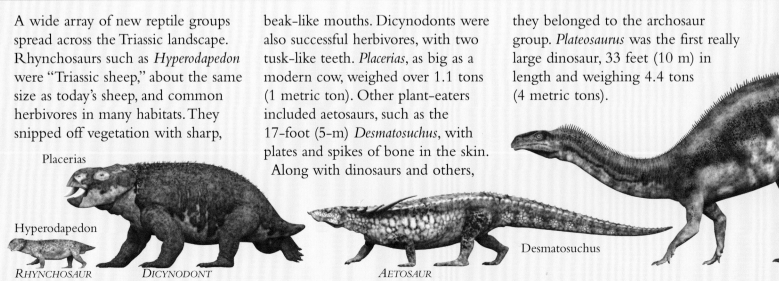

Placerias

Hyperodapedon

Desmatosuchus

RHYNCHOSAUR   DICYNODONT   AETOSAUR

Therapsids continued to develop on land. One of the main groups was the cynodonts, meaning "dog-teeth." They had appeared in the late Permian but evolved several new Triassic groups. Some became very mammal-like, with different-shaped teeth such as canines and molars, warm-blooded bodies, fur, and whiskers. One group, the probainognathians, evolved further. Around 230 to 220 million years ago they had become small, shrew-like insect-eaters—the first true mammals.

Triassic ammonite fossil

In a shallow Triassic sea, massive ichthyosaurs Shonisaurus *(1), 49 feet (15 m) long, munch ammonites, while the protosaurian* Tanystropheus *(2) feeds on jellyfish.* Nothosaurus *(3) and the ichthyosaurs* Cymbospondylus *(4) chase fish.*

Plant life on land also saw rapidly evolving groups, especially seed-bearing trees such as conifers, ginkgoes, and cycads. Seed-ferns, horsetails, and ferns struggled against these newcomers. In seas and oceans, most kinds of fish and invertebrates continued to thrive, although some were reduced by competition with the new marine reptiles.

The Triassic ended much as it began with another of the "Big Five" mass extinctions. About half of all kinds of living things died out over 10–15 million years in this Triassic-Jurassic event. On land the way was clear—for the dinosaurs.

Feasting on the Triassic herbivores were many kinds of predators.

Herrerasaurus, 10 feet (3 m) long, was one of the first dinosaurs, from 231 million years ago in South America. The North American phytosaur *Rutiodon* grew to 16 feet (5 m) and had a crocodile-like lifestyle. In the same region lived *Postosuchus*, a rauisuchian and cousin of true crocodiles, with long, sharp teeth. Avoiding all these carnivores were cynodonts such as *Cynognathus*, which were very close to becoming mammals.

Plateosaurus

Herrerasaurus

DINOSAURS

Rutiodon

PHYTOSAUR

Postosuchus

RAUISUCHIAN

Cynognathus

CYNODONT

JURASSIC
201—145 MILLION YEARS AGO

GREAT CHANGES OCCURRED AROUND THE WORLD DURING THE JURASSIC PERIOD. THE PANGEA SUPERCONTINENT STARTED TO SPLIT IN TWO, ALTERING PATTERNS OF WINDS, OCEAN CURRENTS, AND CLIMATES. HABITATS WERE MORE DIVERSE. IT WAS STILL THE "AGE OF REPTILES," ALTHOUGH ON LAND, A BETTER NAME WAS "AGE OF DINOSAURS."

The biggest bony fish Leedsichthys *(1), 50 feet (15 m), is attacked by* Liopleurodon *(2). A pair of* Ichthyosaurus *(3) compete with a pod of* Plesiosaurus *(4) for fishy food.*

Average world temperatures during the Jurassic were still warm, 63°Fahrenheit (17°Celsius) compared to about 58°F (14.5°C) today. Pangea slowly split in two, Laurasia in the north and Gondwana in the south, creating more coastlines. The climate became damper, deserts shrank, and swamps and forests spread. Many new animals and plants evolved in the growing mix of varied habitats. Grasshoppers, beetles, and other insects became much more common. Many amphibians had disappeared in the Triassic-Jurassic extinction, but salamanders and frogs developed. The few mammals were mostly small and night-active. In the skies, pterosaurs became bigger and more diverse. Toward the end of the Jurassic, new kinds of fliers appeared—birds.

An important difference between dinosaurs and nearly all other reptiles is the legs, which were straight and directly below the body, rather than bent and sprawling sideways as in lizards and crocodiles. This made moving more efficient and faster. The main Jurassic trend for dinosaur evolution was to get bigger. The prosauropod *Anchisaurus* from 190 million years ago was 6.6 feet (2 m) long and weighed 66 pounds (30 kg), while sauropods 50 million years later were 15 times longer and 1,000 times heavier.

Late Jurassic *Europasaurus* was unusual at 20 feet (6 m), probably because it evolved on an island with limited food, known as insular dwarfism.

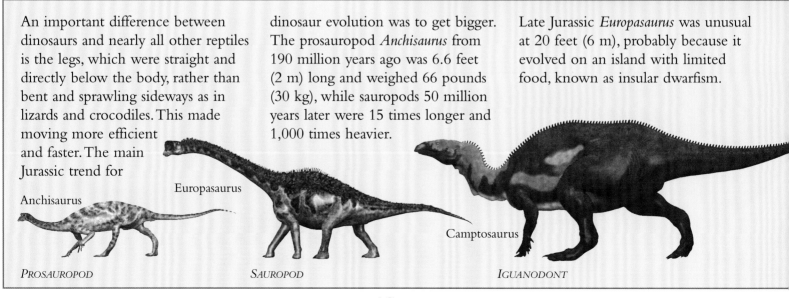

Anchisaurus

Europasaurus

Camptosaurus

PROSAUROPOD   *SAUROPOD*   *IGUANODONT*

By far the most numerous and diverse large land animals were dinosaurs, of which there were three main groups. Theropods were sharp-fanged meat-eaters that stood and ran on their back legs.

A North American Jurassic scene shows Stegosaurus *(1) defending itself from* Ceratosaurus *(2), as* Gargoyleosaurus *(3) trots to safety. On the plains,* Torvosaurus *(4) feasts on an old* Camarasaurus *(5) but is about to be challenged by the larger* Allosaurus *(6). In the background, a mixed group of* Camptosaurus *(7) and* Brachiosaurus *(8) browse on plants as a* Diplodocus *herd (9) moves to new feeding grounds.*

Archaeopteryx was a "dinobird"—a feathered dinosaur in the process of becoming a bird. It was a cousin of modern birds, rather than a direct ancestor.

Sauropods were plant-eaters. They had small heads, long necks and tails, and barrel-shaped bodies. Ornithischians were all herbivores, mostly moving on four legs. Some had horns, spikes, or back plates, while others were covered in bony armor. These groups evolved a variety of sizes, from as small as today's pet cats to giants weighing tens of tons. They dominated the landscape like no other single animal group before or since. At the end of the Jurassic, sauropods such as *Brachiosaurus* were among the biggest animals ever to walk the Earth, exceeding 55 tons (50 metric tons).

In the oceans were more groups of great reptiles. The short-necked plesiosaur *Liopleurodon* measured 33 feet (10 m), with enormous jaws and teeth. Some ichthyosaurs grew nearly as large. Their prey of bony fish, sharks, and ammonites continued to thrive in the warm, wide, shallow Jurassic seas.

Pterosaurs ruled the Jurassic skies. Rhamphorhynchus *(1),* Dimorphodon *(2) and* Pterodactylus *(3) all had wingspans of less than 3 feet (1 m).*

Among ornithopods or "bird-feet," *Camptosaurus* was an iguanodont. At 26 feet (8 m) long, it moved on all-fours or two rear legs. Stegosaurs had tall plates of bone on the back, while ankylosaurs were well armored with bony skin plates. The biggest meat-eaters or theropods included *Yangchuanosaurus* at 33 feet (10 m) in Asia and its North American relative *Allosaurus*. Tiny *Compsognathus* was less than 3.3 feet (1 m).

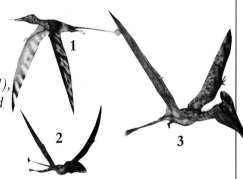

Miragaia,
30 feet (8 m) in length

Gargoyleosaurus

Yangchuanosaurus

Compsognathus

STEGOSAUR

ANKYLOSAUR

LARGE THEROPOD

SMALL THEROPOD

CRETACEOUS
145—66 MILLION YEARS AGO

THE LAST PERIOD OF THE MESOZOIC ERA, "MIDDLE LIFE," WAS AGAIN DOMINATED BY DINOSAURS ON LAND AND OTHER REPTILES IN THE OCEAN. THE TWO HUGE LAND MASSES OF LAURASIA AND GONDWANA CONTINUED TO SPLIT AND DRIFT TO BECOME THE CONTINENTS WE KNOW TODAY. THE CLIMATE TURNED INCREASINGLY VARIED AND SEASONAL.

A feathered Tyrannosaurus roars. Birds take to the sky as bees gather pollen from the newly-evolved flowers. In the foreground, small mammals called Alphadon scurry for cover.

Cretaceous dinosaurs included the immense sauropods, the largest-ever land herbivores, and the theropods, who were the biggest-ever carnivores. More new dinosaur groups appeared. The hadrosaurs or "duck-bills" were named for their wide, flat snouts, like a duck's beak. Hadrosaurs were ornithopods related to the famous *Iguanodon*. They were the most common large herbivores in many northern regions toward the end of the period. Pterosaurs also reached their greatest size ever with *Quetzalcoatlus'* wings spanning 39 feet (12 m). Many more birds appeared in the skies, although they were not the only feathered creatures.

Fossils found since the mid 1990s show various dinosaurs had feathers, especially theropods. The feathers may have developed for display or for body warmth, then later adapted to flight. The stages of evolution from small meat-eating maniraptoran dinosaurs to true birds are difficult to tell apart.

In Cretaceous east Asia, a pair of Caudipteryx *theropods (1) dash in front of a group of* Altirhinus *(2) ornithopods, while the feathered theropod* Microraptor *(3) glides from a cycad. To the right, a* Psittacosaurus *family (4) warily watches the "scythe dinosaur"* Beipiaosaurus *(5).* Zhenyuanopterus *pterosaurs (6), with wings spanning 17 feet (4 m), fly to a river to fish.*

Some dinosaur groups continued from the Jurassic into the Cretaceous. Among them were the heavy-set, well-armored ankylosaurs, including the 20-feet (6-meters), 6.6-tons (6-metric tons) *Ankylosaurus*. One of the biggest meat-eaters was South American *Giganotosaurus*. At 40 feet (13 m) and 8.8 tons (8 metric tons), it was slightly larger than the famous North American *Tyrannosaurus*. Both were outsized by *Spinosaurus*, a swimming, fish-hunting mega-predator from Africa. Its back "sail" was probably for display to impress rivals and mates. The southern sauropods known as titanosaurs grew bigger than in the Jurassic, some reaching around 110 tons (100 metric tons).

Puertasaurus, *one of the largest sauropods, 100 feet (30 m) and 66 tons (60 metric tons)*

Spinosaurus, *biggest-ever land carnivore at 50 feet (15 m) and 9–10 tons (8–9 metric tons)*

Giganotosaurus

Ankylosaurus

CARNOSAUR · ANKYLOSAUR · SPINOSAUR · TITANOSAUR

Quetzalcoatlus *was one of the last and biggest pterosaurs.*

Flowering plants appeared, along with insects such as bees and ants to carry their pollen. Flowers and insects encouraged each other's rapid evolution, known as co-evolution. In the sea, ichthyosaurs went extinct, but another group of huge predatory

The giant sea turtle Archelon *(1) searches for jellyfish as flightless diving birds* Hesperornis *(2) hunt for fish. In the background, the giant mosasaur* Tylosaurus *(3), 50 feet (15 m) long, attacks a plesiosaur* Elasmosaurus *(4).*

reptiles evolved, called the mosasaurs. The period ended when an asteroid smashed into Earth, causing a mass extinction that wiped out three-quarters of all life.

New herbivore groups were the hadrosaurs such as the tall-crested *Parasaurolophus*, 33 feet (10 m), and the ceratopsians or "horn-faces." Largest was *Triceratops*, growing to 30 feet (9 m) and 13 tons (12 metric tons). It was one of the last non-bird dinosaurs, dating to 67–66 million years ago. By this time birds were well established, having evolved from maniraptorans in the late Jurassic.

Deinonychus was a fast and agile 11-feet (3.5-m) long Cretaceous maniraptoran. It lived 110 million years ago. The end-of-Cretaceous mass extinction killed off all non-bird dinosaurs, as well as mosasaurs, plesiosaurs, pterosaurs, and others. It marked the end of both the "Age of Reptiles" and the Mesozoic era.

All dinosaurs, including this sauropod, like all reptiles, hatched from eggs.

Triceratops

Parasaurolophus

Deinonychus

CERATOPSIAN   HADROSAUR   MANIRAPTORAN

PALEOGENE
66—23 MILLION YEARS AGO

THE MASS EXTINCTION AT THE END OF THE CRETACEOUS LEFT THE WORLD A VERY DIFFERENT PLACE. AS LANDSCAPES AND WATERY HABITATS RECOVERED, FOODS FORMERLY EATEN BY THE DINOSAURS AND OTHER REPTILES WERE AVAILABLE TO NEWLY EVOLVING ANIMALS. TWO MAIN GROUPS TOOK ADVANTAGE OF THE OPPORTUNITY—MAMMALS AND BIRDS.

A flightless "terror bird" Diatryma seizes Eohippus, *a small, early form of horse. A pair of early bats,* Icaronycteris, *use their sound-radar (sonar), echolocation, to find insect prey.*

Most of the mammals before the Paleogene were small, less than 16 inches (40 cm) long, shaped like shrews or rats, and probably ate worms, insects, and other bugs. Within 10 million years of the period's start, many new shapes and sizes of mammals had evolved. Herbivores as big as today's rhinos took the place of plant-eating dinosaurs, while wolf-sized predators developed to hunt them. Some of these early mammal groups lasted just a few million years. They were "experiments in evolution." During this time the continents continued to drift apart. The Atlantic Ocean began to widen and separate North and South America from Europe and Africa. This changed winds, sea currents, and rainfall patterns.

The conditions and climate of each continent differed from the others. So, like giant islands, the continents began to evolve their own sets of animals and plants. For example, Australia had drifted away from Antarctica and South America by about 45 million years ago. It still remains separate today, with distinctive flowers, insects, and pouched mammals called marsupials, found nowhere else.

A pack of Daeodon *"hell pigs" (1) watch the biggest-ever land mammal* Paraceratherium *(2) bond with her calf. Behind grazes a herd of* Menoceras *(3), that are also rhinos.*

Darwinius

The primate mammal group includes lemurs, bushbabies, monkeys, apes, and humans. Primate fossils are known from around 55 million years ago. One of the most complete is *Darwinius*, 24 inches (60 cm) long and 47 million years old, with soft

parts such as skin and fur preserved. Similar small animals were probably prey to *Titanoboa*, the largest snake known, 43 feet (13 m) in length, from 58 million years ago. Another massive predator was *Andrewsarchus*,

Titanoboa

An Andrewsarchus *duo stalk a freshwater turtle.*

a mammal that was 13 feet (4 m) long. However it was more closely related to hippos and pigs than to today's carnivorous mammals.

Size guide

Three Moeritherium, *early relations of elephants, munch lake plants, watched by more hoofed herbivores,* Arsinoitherium.

By the middle of the Paleogene, most of the main mammal groups known today had appeared. Bats took to the air, with front limbs that had become wings. Seals' and sea-lions' legs evolved into flippers so the animals could feed in the sea, although they remained on land to breed. Whales became fully adapted to the ocean. Their front limbs developed

into flippers, their back limbs almost disappeared, and their tail evolved with flukes, wide flaps for swimming. The first whales were predatory and filled the role left empty when the plesiosaur and mosasaur reptiles disappeared. The only sea reptiles left after the mass extinction were sea turtles. Most other groups of sea animals were still present. Bony fish continued to evolve and diversify rapidly with thousands of new species. Sharks, squid, and others also developed new species, but their shapes and

Basilosaurus *was one of the first whales. Huge at 60 feet (18 m) in length, it lived about 40 million years ago.*

features remained similar to how they were 300 million years earlier.

Mammals were not the only new, big land animals. Several groups of huge, powerful birds appeared. They had strong legs and big beaks, but tiny, useless wings. Some birds were herbivores, eating fast-evolving flowers, seeds, and fruits. Others, known as the "terror birds," were fearsome hunters.

Megacerops was a large, heavy, herbivorous ungulate, or hoofed mammal, 16 feet (5 m) long, that lived in North America 38 million years ago. It was a brontothere, a

Megacerops

cousin of rhinos. But all brontotheres died out a few million years later, perhaps faced with competition from lighter, faster ungulates such as the horse family. These early ungulates were likely prey of creodonts, predatory mammals that appeared just 3–5 million years after the great extinction. Creodonts evolved into many forms, shaped like today's cats, dogs, wolves, and bears. Some took to crunching towershells and other shellfish along the coasts. However all creodonts died out by 10 million

years ago, again probably due to competition, this time from the Carnivora—the living cats, dogs, wolves, bears, stoats, mongooses, and other mammal carnivores.

fossil Turritella *towershell, a type of sea-snail*

NEOGENE
23—2.58 MILLION YEARS AGO

Second period of the Mesozoic era, "recent life," the Neogene was marked by further evolution of land mammals. Many mammmals still familiar today appeared—including the first humans. The Neogene ended with the first of the recent ice ages, as the world cooled and glaciers spread across northern lands.

On the plains of Africa 3 million years ago, two Australopithecus, *our hominid cousins, avoid a pair of 9-ton (8-metric ton), four-tusked elephants,* Stegotetrabelodon.

Fossils have formed throughout Earth's history. As time passed, more and more fossils were destroyed by continental drift, volcanic eruptions, earthquakes, and erosion (wearing away of rocks). So as time periods became more recent, fossils were more plentiful. During the Neogene the fossils show living things evolving into the familiar kinds of today. Among plants, grasses probably appeared at the end of the Cretaceous, but the slowly drying, cooling climate of the Neogene meant they spread over much larger areas. New kinds of herbivores evolved to graze them, rather than browsing leaves in the shrinking woods and forests. Grasslands were also home to insects

such as grasshoppers and termites. In east Africa, another effect of fewer woodlands was that some primates in the great ape group, hominids, spent less time in trees and more time on the ground. From about 5 million years ago they gradually adapted to walking more upright on two legs, leaving their hands free to gather food and, later, to use tools.

Platybelodon *(1) and* Deinotherium *(2), relatives of the modern elephants, both graze and browse in the grassy woodlands of Asia 10 million years ago.*

On the evolutionary "tree" of life, it is estimated that the branch leading to humans probably split from the chimpanzee branch 6 to 7 million years ago in Africa. Fossils from the human line soon after this are rare until around 5 million years ago, with the appearance of five or more kinds of *Australopithecus*, or "southern ape." At the end of the Neogene or soon after, one of these gave rise to our own human group, *Homo*. Some of the most beautiful Neogene fossils are found in the gold-colored,

"Lucy," an Australopithecus afarensis *hominid, lived in northeast Africa about 3.2 million years ago. Her well-preserved fossils allow a lifelike reconstruction and showed she was 53 inches (110 cm) tall and walked almost upright.*

Amber (right) contains perfect fossils, such as this mosquito (above).

hardened plant resin called amber. It oozed from certain conifer trees to trap and preserve creatures such as spiders, frogs, lizards, and mice in amazing detail.

Kyptoceras walks cautiously through a forest in what is now Florida, North America, some 5 million years ago. It was an extinct form of living chevrotains or mouse-deer.

Megalodon *tooth (half actual size)*

Some 10 million years ago the biggest-ever shark Megalodon, *59 feet (18 m) long and 55 tons (50 metric tons), attacks* Zygophyseter, *a toothed whale about half its size.*

The huge, flightless, predatory "terror birds" of the Paleogene had almost died out, although some very large, non-flying, herbivorous birds remained on isolated islands. The main large animals were now mammals. These included elephants and rhinos on land, whales, dolphins, and seals in the seas, and bats in the air. Birds also became more diverse, with all modern groups present, from hummingbirds to eagles. The largest known flying bird, *Pelagornis*,

soared over oceans 25 million years ago. Its wingspan exceeded 23 feet (7 m). As it swooped to feed at the surface, tooth-like spikes along its bill gripped fish and other slippery prey.

Sharks were the biggest sea fish, including the largest ever of the group, *Megalodon*. Big predatory bony fish also appeared, such as marlin and swordfish. As some continents drifted north or south into cooler waters, their shoreline habitats became more varied, with new kinds of seaweeds such as kelps. Animals adapted to feed on and shelter among them—crabs and other crustaceans, and shellfish molluscs such as sea-snails and clams.

The appearance of kelp and other brown seaweeds in cooler waters changed many shores. These plants grew to great sizes and formed "underwater forests" that were home to myriad small creatures, from shrimps to fish. Mammals such as sea otters, and sirenians, similar to the present day Australian dugong, also adapted to kelp forests. Also in Australia marsupials adapted to grasslands and eucalypt woods. They included the largest land mammal predator, the thylacine or "marsupial wolf."

Kelps grow as big as trees on land.

Brachiopod or lampshell fossils from 15 million years ago are similar to their earliest relatives of 500 million years ago.

Thylacines were carnivorous marsupials.

PLEISTOCENE
2,588,000—11,700 YEARS AGO

THE PLEISTOCENE WAS A TIME OF REPEATED ICE AGES OR GLACIATIONS. THE WORLD MAP WOULD LOOK FAMILIAR TO US, WITH LAND MASSES IN THEIR MODERN POSITIONS. BUT SEA LEVELS VARIED WIDELY. THEY FELL WITH COOL TEMPERATURES AS WATER WAS LOCKED UP IN ICE CAPS AND GLACIERS. THEY ROSE IN WARM SPELLS OR INTERGLACIALS.

In Africa 2 million years ago, a group of the first humans, Homo habilis, *butcher a carcass using stone tools.*

A great force in the natural world is temperature. As it dropped at the start of a Pleistocene ice age, glaciers and ice sheets spread out from the poles and down from mountains. Near these ice fronts, warm-blooded animals had to adapt, with thicker mammal fur and more bird feathers to keep out the cold. Another adaptation was larger body size. A big body keeps in heat more effectively than a small one. This led to huge mammoths, rhinos, bears, big cats, and other Pleistocene megafauna, or "great animals." As the cold deepened, habitats with their plants and animals were gradually pushed toward the tropics, where forests shrank and cool grasslands spread. When the glaciation faded, all these changes reversed. This happened up to a dozen times as the Pleistocene's main ice ages came and went. At the coldest time, ice covered one-third of planet Earth, although the effects were less in the southern half of the world since it has much less land.

Two Homo erectus, *a formerly widespread human species, are cutting up a deer while trying to scare away a saber-toothed cat, in this Asian scene around a million years ago.*

The human story began in Africa about 2.8 million years ago and involved walking more upright, growing taller, with a bigger brain and better tools. All humans belong to the genus (group of closely related species) *Homo*, "man" or "person." The first was probably *H. habilis*, "handy man," in east Africa. Simple stone tools such as scrapers and choppers have been found with its fossils, although its brain was less than half the size of modern people. *H. ergaster*, "working man," was taller, with a larger brain and more varied, carefully shaped tools. It may have spread from Africa to Asia. *H. erectus*, "upright man," was even larger, about as tall as humans today and with a brain around two-thirds the size of modern people. It spread from Africa into Europe and across Asia. Some of its fossils from China were formerly known as "Peking (Beijing) Man," and from southeast Asia as "Java Man."

Homo erectus

Homo ergaster

Homo habilis

In South America 1 million years ago, a giant ground sloth Megatherium *(1) has wandered into a pack of saber-toothed cats* Smilodon *(2) attempting to kill a giant armadillo* Glyptodon *(3).*

together, there were winners and losers. For example, saber-toothed cats *Smilodon,* had evolved in the north. As they spread south, they hunted and killed off many kinds of South American prey. This land bridge also separated the Pacific and Atlantic oceans. Sea creatures that had wandered between the two, such as fish, whales, dolphins, and seals, began to evolve their own distinct kinds in these now-separate oceans.

As Pleistocene sea levels went up and down by 330 feet (100 m) or more, some areas of land were cut off, then rejoined by land bridges. This allowed plants and animals to evolve in isolated areas, then mix and face competition from new species, which led to further changes. One of the main land bridges, the Isthmus of Panama, joined the continents of North and South America. When their different sets of animals and plants came

A hunting scene 100,000 years ago in ice-age Europe shows Homo neanderthalensis *lying in wait as a group of woolly mammoths strides past a pair of feeding woolly rhinos.*

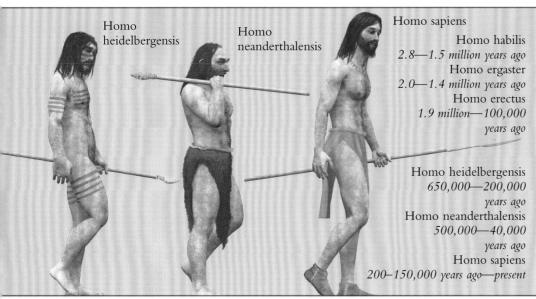

Homo heidelbergensis

Homo neanderthalensis

Homo sapiens

Homo habilis
2.8—1.5 million years ago
Homo ergaster
2.0—1.4 million years ago
Homo erectus
1.9 million—100,000 years ago

Homo heidelbergensis
650,000—200,000 years ago
Homo neanderthalensis
500,000—40,000 years ago
Homo sapiens
200–150,000 years ago—present

H. heidelbergensis, named after a fossil jaw from Heidelberg, Germany, probably evolved from *H. erectus*. Its brain was almost the size of modern humans. In Europe and Asia, it gave rise to *H. neanderthalensis*, also named from German fossils, from the Neander Valley. This muscular, strong species survived most, but not all, of the last Pleistocene ice ages. Then in Africa around 200–150,000 years ago, *H. heidelbergensis* probably evolved into our own species, *H. sapiens*, "wise man."

HOLOCENE
11,700 YEARS AGO—TODAY

THE HOLOCENE FOLLOWED THE PLEISTOCENE AS THE SECOND EPOCH OF THE MOST RECENT PERIOD, THE QUATERNARY. IT BEGAN WITH THE FADING OF THE LAST ICE AGE. DURING ITS TIME HUMANS DEVELOPED FARMING WITH SPECIALLY BRED CROPS AND LIVESTOCK, CREATED CIVILIZATIONS, BUILT CITIES, AND HUGELY ALTERED THE WORLD'S HABITATS AND BALANCE OF NATURE.

As the last ice age ended, and the glaciers and ice sheets melted back, plants and animals spread north and south again as regions became newly habitable. However many of the great ice-age "megafauna" mammals were already extinct or almost so. The causes were probably rapid climate warming, which caused their cold grassland habitats to shrink, and the spread of humans to every continent except Antarctica. Cave and rock art show hunting scenes, and the bones of woolly mammoths, woolly rhinos and others have cut marks where they were butchered with stone tools.

The last woolly mammoths on mainland Asia

The dodo, a flightless bird on the island of Mauritius, was extinct by 1700 due to hunting, habitat loss, and introduced species.

lived around 10,000 years ago. About this time, farm crops were already being harvested in west Asia, in the region of modern-day Syria, Iraq, and Iran.

The impact of humans, from hunting to climate change, has contributed to the disappearance of most "megafauna" on all continents except for small areas of Africa—where humans first evolved.

Explorers and naturalists such as Henry Bates (1825–1892, left) collected animals and plants to help our understanding of the natural world. Zoos (above) began as simple viewing galleries for strange beasts, but they now help to save and breed rare species.

For centuries, people regarded nature as "inexhaustible." They hunted wild animals, felled forests, dug mines and quarries, and fished the oceans with little thought to long-term effects. From the 1760s, the Industrial Revolution, fast-growing cities, and rising human populations increased the need for natural resources. Problems began to grow, such as pollution of air and water, along with more species going extinct. Some people realized the harm and started to work toward protecting nature.

Wildlife in all habitats, from oceans to tropical forests, faces threats such as fishing, farming, and pollution.

The first major human civilizations were also in west Asia and in northeast Africa, where ancient Egyptians began building cities and pyramids 5,000 years ago. More civilizations developed in China, India, parts of Africa, and Central America. Since then, humans have spread and increased in numbers to billions. They have taken over vast areas of land for food, industry, living, and leisure. This has shrunk or destroyed many wild habitats along with their plants and animals. Some experts say that, added to the previous "Big Five" extinctions, Earth is now undergoing its sixth, the Holocene mass extinction, due to human activities.

Rare plants, such as the well-known mountain edelweiss (Leontopodium alpinum), a member of the daisy family, are protected in many countries.

National parks protect the landscape, habitats, plants, and animals. One of the first was Yosemite, USA, founded in the 1870s.

In the 1800s, some nations began setting aside protected areas as nature reserves and national parks. During the 1900s, scientists began to identify environmental problems such as acid rain, the thinning of the ozone layer in Earth's atmosphere, and global warming due to greenhouse gases from burning fuels. Illegal hunting, collecting, and poaching of rare species continues. Not only people, but all of life on Earth must cope with these enormous challenges in the future.

GLOSSARY

amniotes
Animals that lay eggs with tough, waterproof shells, that can survive on land. They include reptiles, birds, and mammals.

arthropod
An invertebrate animal with a hard outer body casing (exoskeleton) and jointed legs. This huge and varied group includes insects, spiders, millipedes, centipedes, crabs and other crustaceans, trilobites, eurypterids or sea scorpions, and many others.

bony fish
A fish with a skeleton made partly or completely of bones.

Cambrian explosion
The time between about 540 and 515 million years ago when a wide variety of living things evolved rapidly in the seas, including early forms of many animal groups that still survive today.

co-evolution
When two groups of living things evolve together, so that they depend or rely largely on each other, for example, insects and flowers during the Cretaceous Period.

continental drift
The very slow moving or sliding of the Earth's major land masses across its surface, on their huge, curved, jigsaw-like slabs of rock known as tectonic plates.

eons
The largest divisions or time spans in the history of Earth, such as the Hadean and Archean. Eons are divided into eras.

epochs
The fourth-largest divisions or time spans in the history of Earth, such as the Pleistocene and Holocene.

eras
The second-largest divisions or time spans in the history of Earth, such as the Paleozoic, Mesozoic and Cenozoic. Eras are divided into periods.

eukaryotes
Single living cells with some parts inside wrapped in skin-like membranes, such as the genetic material in the nucleus. Compare *prokaryote*.

evolution
The changes in living things that take place over time, as they become more suited or adapted to their environment.

extinction
When a particular kind or group of living things dies out completely and no longer exists. Extinctions can affect a species, genus or larger group, and may be in a certain region or worldwide. See also *mass extinction*.

fossils
The remains of living things preserved in the rocks, altered by minerals and "turned to stone." Hard parts are most likely to fossilize such as roots, bark, cones and nuts, and animal shells, bones and teeth.

genus
A group of closely related species, with the same first part of their two-part scientific name. For example, the genus *Homo*, humans, includes the living species *Homo sapiens*, modern humans, also the extinct *Homo neanderthalensis*, Neanderthal people, *Homo erectus*, "upright man," and several other species.

habitat
A particular kind of environment or surroundings, such as a woodland, desert, mountain, lake, river, swamp, sandy shore, rocky coast, or deep seabed.

invertebrate
An animal without a backbone or vertebral column. Invertebrates are hugely varied, from jellyfish, corals and worms to molluscs like ammonites, snails and squid, and arthropods.

lobe-fins
Fish with fins that have a muscular stump-like base, rather than stiff rods or spines as in ray-fins.

mass extinction
When most kinds of living things (typically more than half) die out completely over a relatively short time period, usually a few million years or less.

ornithischians
One of the main groups of dinosaurs, mostly plant-eaters that walked on all four legs. They had a wide variety of shapes and features, such as bony plates, spikes, horns, frills, and beak-like mouths.

periods
The third-largest divisions or time spans in the history of Earth, such as the Cambrian, Triassic and Neogene. Periods are divided into epochs.

prokaryotes
The simplest living things, each is a single microscopic cell with the parts inside floating freely. Compare *eukaryote*.

sauropods
One of the main groups of dinosaurs, typically plant-eaters with a small head, very long neck and tail, wide tubby body, and four straight, column-shaped, elephant-like legs.

seed
In plants, a tiny baby or embryo plant with a food store for its early growth, inside a tough outer casing. Compare *spore*.

species
A group of very similar living things who look alike and can breed together to produce offspring, who can then breed together.

spore
In plants, a tiny baby or embryo plant inside a tough outer casing. Compare *seed*.

synapsids
Vertebrate animals with a particular pattern of openings or gaps in the skull, specifically one opening low down behind the eye. They include the extinct pelycosaurs and therapsids ("mammal-like reptiles") and the mammals.

tetrapods
Four-limbed vertebrate animals, including living amphibians, reptiles, birds, and mammals, and their extinct relatives.

theropods
One of the main groups of dinosaurs, who were mostly meat-eaters or predators, and usually walked on their two back legs, using the front limbs as "arms."

vertebrate
An animal with a backbone or vertebral column, including most fish, and all amphibians, reptiles, birds, mammals, and their extinct relatives.

INDEX